CONTENTS

THE RAILWAY AGE

It was September 1851 and ten-year-old Laura Watson was too excited to sleep. Her trunk was packed and tomorrow she was going on holiday. Laura lived in Newcastle-upon-Tyne and was to travel by train with her father and governess to see the Great Exhibition in London. After visiting the city her father had promised they would take a few quiet days by the sea in Brighton.

Queen Victoria reigned from 1837-1901. During her long rule Britain became the leading industrial country in the world and built a huge overseas empire. Historians call this vibrant time the Victorian era. The Victorians were the first high-tech society. They lived in an age of rapid technological change and nothing showed this more than the breathtaking spread of the railways.

(*Right*) The rail network in 1851, the year of Laura's journey. Her route is highlighted.

4

George Stephenson built the first proper railway from Stockton to Darlington. This opened in 1825 and ran for 43 km (27 miles). It was built to carry coal but ran one, horse-powered, passenger train a day. Before the Stockton-Darlington line was even finished, Stephenson was planning a bolder scheme. In 1830 he completed the first steam passenger railway, from Liverpool to Manchester. In 18 months it carried 700,000 people and made a hefty profit.

George Stephenson was the first great railway engineer. He designed, surveyed and built complete railways, from laying the tracks to manufacturing the locomotives.

Soon a web of railways began to link Britain's major cities and ports. The line from London to Birmingham opened in 1838 and the link to Gateshead, just across the River Tyne from Newcastle, was completed by 1844. When Victoria became queen there were about 1,400 miles (2,300 kilometres) of railway track. When she died this had soared to 20,000 miles (32,000 kilometres).

Most railways around the world are 4 feet 6 inches (1.3 metres) wide. This was the distance between the wheels of coal wagons in the mines of north-east England, where George Stephenson learned his trade. He used the same width on his railway lines and set a standard that most other engineers followed.

THE INDUSTRIAL REVOLUTION

The following morning Laura woke early, but had to wait patiently for her father. He owned a rope works on the banks of the River Tyne and had gone to see that all was well before he left for London. Newcastle was a thriving city and Mr Watson sold ropes to shipyards and mines across northern England.

The growth of Victorian towns was even more astonishing than the spread of the railways. In 1750 most people lived and worked in the countryside. Over the next 100 years, this traditional lifestyle was turned upside down by a wave of new ideas and inventions. Historians call this the Industrial Revolution.

'Locomotives in every stage of progress meet the eyes on every side. When we reflect that each machine contains more than 5,000 pieces of metal and costs about £2,000 and that one railway company has 500 such machines, can we fail to be impressed?'

A DESCRIPTION OF THE STEPHENSON LOCOMOTIVE WORKS IN NEWCASTLE, 1855.

All over the country small market towns turned into booming centres of industry as factories, ironworks, chemical plants and shipyards were built. Different communities became famous for different products: Manchester for cotton mills and cloth; Sheffield for steel; Stoke-on-Trent for pottery and china; and Birmingham for engineering and metal-working.

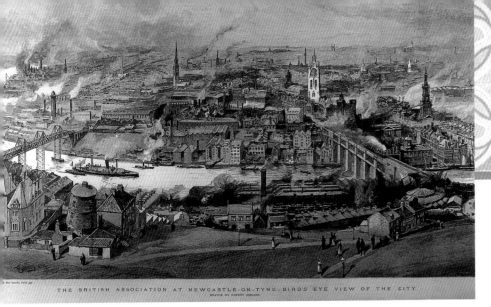

A bird's eye view of Newcastle in 1889.

Newcastle became a centre of the coal trade. But by 1851 there were many industries in the city too — brewing, brick making, iron and lead works, shipbuilding, glass making and, of course, locomotive building.

Many of the products made in Britain were sold abroad and the country became rich – as this advert for a Sheffield firm shows. No wonder the Victorians proudly boasted that they lived in the 'workshop of the world'.

CONSTANTINE BROTHERS,
MERCHANTS, AND MANUFACTURERS OF ALL KINDS OF
SAWS, FILES, STEEL,
Suitable for the United States, Canadian, the British Colonies, and Continental Markets;
CALICO WEBS, MACHINE KNIVES, LEDGER BLADES, SPIRAL CUTTERS, &c.,
68 & 70, HOLLIS CROFT, SHEFFIELD.

Manufacturers of the celebrated Goods marked
CONSTANTINE BROTHERS
C.B
SHEFFIELD.
F. CONSTANTINE.
BATTISON & CO.
I. COLBECK.
PORTERS.

City	1801	1851	1871
Birmingham	71,000	233,000	344,000
Glasgow	77,000	345,000	522,000
Newcastle	33,000	88,000	128,000
Manchester	75,000	303,000	351,000
London	959,000	2,362,000	3,254,000

The population of most cities soared during the Victorian era, as this table shows:

In 1851 the census recorded a momentous change. The population of Britain had reached nearly 21 million. And, for the first time, more than half lived in towns and cities, not the countryside.

DEADLY TOWNS

Laura passed the time, until her father returned, reading with her governess in the nursery. Laura lived in Summerhill, a square of big terraced houses with a private park. She lived a wealthy and privileged life in a comfortable home, with servants to look after her. She knew little of the dirt and squalor in which many poorer people spent their lives.

The one-room home of a London costermonger, a street trader, in 1872.

Industry had brought wealth to some Victorians, but lives of misery to others. The new towns grew so quickly that they were grim places to live. Terraces of cheap houses were built close to factories and workshops. Most had no drains or running water and were often damp and cold.

The streets were not paved and were usually full of rubbish. Factory chimneys belched out filthy smoke, polluting the atmosphere and blocking out the light. Diseases like cholera and typhoid were rife and killed thousands, especially children. Newcastle was well known as one of the most crowded and unhealthy cities in Britain.

'In the sewers of Newcastle, boys from 10 years of age combine amusement and profit by rat catching. One boy will take from four to eight rats and sell them for 2d or 3d (1-1 $^1/_2$p) each, according to size. They are bought by persons who resell them at about 6d (2 $^1/_2$p) to be worried by dogs!'

MR WILLIAM LEE, INSPECTOR OF THE BOARD OF HEALTH, 1853

In 1851 about 1 million people worked as servants. The most common job for a girl in Newcastle was domestic servant. Victorian servants in the 1850s were poorly paid: housemaids earned £12-£14 a year and cooks £11-£17 a year. This is just over £1 a month. A pair of well-made boots would have cost about 10 shillings, so a servant would have had to save up to afford a pair.

As town centres became over-crowded, richer middle-class families, like Laura's, moved to the outskirts, or suburbs. They lived in detached villas or terraces of large houses with gardens and plenty of fresh air. To run their homes they hired servants: housemaids, nurserymaids, cooks, valets, gardeners and grooms. In the 1850s a man who earned £1,000 a year could easily afford six servants.

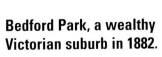

Bedford Park, a wealthy Victorian suburb in 1882.

HORSE POWER

At last it was time to go. Tom, the groom, drove the horses and carriage to the front of the house and loaded the trunks. Laura watched her father smiling as they pulled away. He was pleased that he could afford to keep a carriage. 'It impresses the neighbours, shopkeepers and customers, my girl. It shows them we are carriage people.'

Railways caught the imagination of the Victorians, but for everyday transport they relied on horses to pull passengers and goods.

A rich London family in their carriage in 1867.

Wealthy families like Laura's kept a two-horse, four-wheel carriage like a landau or a barouche. But even a one-horse carriage, like a gig, was enough to show the high standing of the owner. In 1856 around 200,000 people kept a private carriage.

Coaches from Newcastle to Gateshead

BELSAY.—A coach leaves the Lowther Inn, Newgate St., every Tues.,Thurs., and Sat. at 4 p.m.

BLACKHILL.—A coach leaves the White Swan Inn, Cloth Market, every afternoon at 6.

CONSETT AND LEADGATE.—A coach leaves the White Swan Inn, Cloth Market, every afternoon at 4.

CONSETT.—A coach leaves the White Swan Inn, Cloth Market, every morning at 7.

DIPTON.—A coach leaves the White Swan Inn, Cloth Market, every afternoon at 4.

OTTERBURN.—A coach (carrying the mail bags), leaves the Garrick's Head, Cloth Market, every morning at 7. Carries no passengers.

PONTELAND.—A van leaves the Phœnix Inn, Newgate Street, Tuesdays, Thursdays, and Saturdays at 4 p.m.

SHOTLEY.—A coach leaves the White Swan Inn, every afternoon at 6.

STAMFORDHAM.—A coach leaves the Victoria Hotel, Newgate Street, every Tuesday, Thursday, and Saturday at 4 p.m.

WHALTON.—A van leaves the Phœnix Inn, Newgate Street, every Tuesday, Thursday, and Saturday at 4 p.m.

WHITTINGTON AND STAMFORDHAM.—A coach leaves the Victoria Hotel, Newgate Street, every Tuesday and Saturday at 4 p.m.

A coach timetable from _Christie's Directory of Newcastle and Gateshead_, 1874.

Carrier wagons moved heavy goods and parcels to places the railways did not reach, or to and from stations or ports. Drawn by eight or more horses, depending on the load, they were the heavy goods lorries of their day. The first horse buses — known as omnibuses — were used in London in 1829 and the idea quickly spread to other large towns. There were even traffic jams as city streets became busy with carts delivering everything from coal and ice to milk and bread.

Railways caused a cut in the use of horses for long distance travel but led to an increase in local use. The number of working horses doubled between 1850 and 1902 to 3.5 million. By 1903 London had 4,000 horse buses carrying 500 million people every year.

This painting, dated 1850, is called _Past and Present Through Victorian Eyes_. It shows the fate of long distance stage-coaches – too slow and expensive to compete with trains.

RAILWAY STATIONS

S oon they pulled up at the bustling station and Tom went to seek a porter. Laura marvelled at the elegant building, opened only a year ago by Queen Victoria. Soon Tom returned to say the train was waiting at the platform. With the help of a porter, he lifted the trunks on to the roof of a first class carriage, while the others stepped aboard.

This painting, *Paddington Station, London*, by W P Firth shows the excitement and colour of a Victorian station in 1802.

Railway stations fascinated Victorians. They brought people of all classes together — from Dukes to chimney sweeps. Nothing like this had ever happened before! And though the wealthy bought first-class tickets and ordinary people third-class — they would all travel at the same speed.

Large stations were built to impress travellers. The Victorians believed that railways were the greatest achievement of

Newcastle Central Station was built in the classical style, with a dramatic portico 200 feet (61m) long and 50 feet (15m) wide at the front. But the train shed behind was very modern – the roof had three huge arches of wrought iron and glass, held up by iron pillars. Notice the horse-drawn trams.

the human mind and wanted to celebrate them in stone, iron and glass. Euston Station, opened in 1837 for the London and Birmingham Railway, set a high standard. It had a huge portico (porch) — like something out of ancient Athens. Even small stations were built with features borrowed from Greek temples or medieval castles.

Inside, stations were as busy as markets. Most had a small army of uniformed staff: porters, ticket clerks and signalmen and a station-master. Alongside the booking-office, waiting-rooms and toilets there might be a hotel, a buffet, a bar, a book stall, a hairdresser and a host of shops.

"It appears to me that Rail Roads are the Vulgarest, most injurious to Health of any mode of conveyance [transport]. Mobs of well dressed Ladies and Gentlemen are collected at every station, to examine and pry into every Carriage and the actions of every Traveller."

THE DUKE OF WELLINGTON, 1848

In the 1850s railway carriages still looked like horse-drawn vehicles: stagecoaches with padded seats for first class and plainer wagons with hard wooden seats for third class. The luggage was stored on top and sometimes caught fire if hot ashes blew back from the engine.

13

BUILDING RAILWAYS

Her father smiled at Laura as the train puffed slowly out of the station. 'My dear, you are about to see one of the most impressive views in the world — the River Tyne from Robert Stephenson's High Level Bridge. The great works of our railway engineers take my breath away.' Laura pressed her nose against the window, she didn't want to miss a thing.

The High Level Bridge in Newcastle was designed by Robert Stephenson and opened in 1849. It brought the main line from London into the heart of Newcastle. The road and rail decks were made of cast iron.

Railway engineers were celebrities in the 1850s. Everyone knew the names of men like Robert Stephenson (George's son — and an even better engineer than his dad!) and Isambard Kingdom Brunel. In command of armies of workers called 'navvies', their railway lines ripped through the countryside with great cuttings, viaducts and bridges.

Navvies worked hard, with few machines to help them. Their tools were picks, shovels and wheelbarrows. A good navvy was expected to shovel about 20 tonnes of earth a day.

Brunel was a strong-minded genius who could turn his hand to any engineering task — from steamships to docks. He was only 27 when he was appointed engineer to the Great Western Railway (GWR) and set out to build a new, faster railway — with broad gauge track 7 feet (2.1 metres) instead of 4 feet 6 inches (1.3 metres).

Many of the first railway labourers learned their skills building canals. They were called navigators and got the nickname 'navvies'. By 1847 there were about 255,000 navvies building railways.

He surveyed the line, bargained with landowners to cross their property, designed the tunnels, bridges and stations — and for good measure he drew up the specifications for engines and carriages. By May 1845 the service from London to Exeter was the fastest in the world.

TRAVELLING BY TRAIN

The journey to London took over ten hours. The train stopped for a refreshment break at York and Laura's father bought them all hot mutton pies and tea from a platform vendor. The journey went smoothly until they were pulling into Lincoln. Then, the engine broke down and it was an hour before a new locomotive arrived.

Even for first-class passengers a Victorian railway journey could be uncomfortable. Each carriage was divided into compartments but there were no corridors. And no buffet cars — or toilets! The only heating in winter came from foot-warmers — metal flasks filled with hot water. Lighting was very poor, with a single oil lamp in each compartment. Passengers who wanted to read brought their own candles. Trains took long stops at some larger stations so that passengers could buy food and visit the toilet.

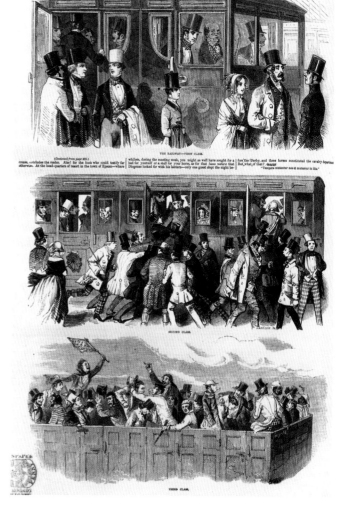

Three classes of travel on the Manchester to Liverpool railway.

Safety features were slow to improve too. At first, signals had depended upon men stationed along the track waving flags but as the number of lines, points and junctions grew, a better system was needed.

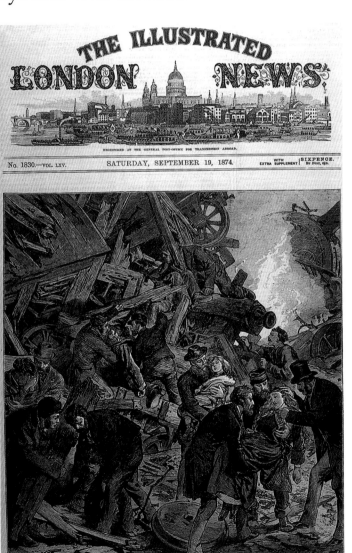

By the 1850s groups of mechanical signals were controlled by one man in a signal box and signalmen were able to send messages about train times to one another using the telegraph (see page 25). But signals were no use if the train couldn't stop in time. It was not until 1889, after a terrible crash in Armagh, Northern Ireland killed 78 people, that the government forced companies to fit efficient brakes.

The night mail and night express of the Great Eastern Railway crashed head-on at Thorpe, outside Norwich in 1874. Twenty-two passengers and crew were killed.

ARRIVING IN LONDON

Laura woke as the train pulled into Maiden Lane station. Two porters carried their heavy trunks to a Hansom cab. The ride to their hotel was slow. The roads were so busy that Laura could only marvel at the crowds. She had never seen so many people earning a living on the streets — and was shocked to see that lots of them were children.

This drawing *Over London by Rail*, by Gustave Doré, shows the backyards of terraced houses in a slum area of the capital, 1875.

London was not only the largest city in Victorian Britain, it was the largest in the western world. At its core was the old City of London, the Square Mile, and alongside, the City of Westminster, the 'West End'. In 1851 many merchants still lived with their families above their counting houses and the streets were busy with shops, slaughter houses and workshops. But already new suburbs flourished along the tentacles of roads and railways that led to the centre — among them Bayswater and Bethnal Green north of the Thames, and Walworth and Camberwell to the south.

A young crossing sweeper touches his forelock as a wealthy lady passes, in this painting by W P Firth, 1855.

Yet it was not just the size of London that fascinated visitors — it was a city of harsh contrasts. The wealthy lived in elegant Georgian squares, while the teeming slums, the 'rookeries', festered close by. The great city banks loaned money to support the nation's trade with the rest of the world, while abandoned children begged in the streets. Parliament decided the affairs of the empire but the MPs sat behind closed windows to keep out the stink of the black and polluted River Thames.

To visitors, London seemed full of Hansom cabs – horse-drawn taxis based on a design made in 1834 by Joseph Aloysius Hansom. His 'safety cabs' had large wheels and low slung bodies to reduce injuries to passengers. There were about 4,600 cab drivers in London by 1861 and they had a reputation for being criminals and drunks.

THE CRYSTAL PALACE

The next day Laura, her father and governess caught a cab to Hyde Park to visit the Great Exhibition. As they walked through the gates Laura gasped. She had read about the wonderful Crystal Palace but had not realized how beautiful it was. When the sun shone on the glass walls she thought it was like a scene from the *Arabian Nights*. Throngs of visitors were already queuing to enter.

Raising the ribs of the transept (the main aisle covered by a dome) roof, during the building of the Crystal Palace in December 1850.

The Great Exhibition was an idea of Prince Albert, the husband of Queen Victoria. He wanted to celebrate the achievements of British and foreign industry. There had been industrial shows before, especially in France, but the Great Exhibition was to be the largest ever held.

The site chosen by the planners was Hyde Park, then on the outskirts of London. Joseph Paxton created a spectacular design for the exhibition building — soon nicknamed the Crystal Palace. Paxton drafted the first sketches on a piece of blotting paper while he was waiting for a train. Only nine days later the full drawings were ready. Brilliantly, his structure was made of

A Poem to Celebrate the Crystal Palace

But yesterday a naked sod
The dandies sneered from Rotten Row
And cantered o'er it two and fro;
And see 'tis done!
As though 'twere by a wizard's rod
A blazing arch of lucid glass
Leaps like a fountain from the grass
To meet the sun!

WILLIAM MAKEPEACE THACKERY, 1851

● The Crystal Palace looked like a giant conservatory. It was 610 metres long and 120 metres wide. Some of the trees already growing on the site were left to grow inside.

● There were 1,060 iron columns, supporting 2,224 girders and 358 trusses, forty kilometres of guttering and 300 kilometres of sash bar. The columns were hollow so that they could be used as drain-pipes when it rained.

● After the Great Exhibition the Crystal Palace was taken down and rebuilt at Sydenham Hill in South London. It was eventually destroyed by a fire in 1936.

prefabricated iron and glass. The pieces were made in factories and the building put together on site. Work did not begin until August 1850 but everything was ready for Queen Victoria to open the Great Exhibition on 1 May 1851.

Queen Victoria opens the Great Exhibition on 1 May 1851.

THE GREAT EXHIBITION

As they walked back to the hotel, Laura and her father discussed the exhibition. 'What did you enjoy most?' he asked. Laura thought hard. 'The Koh-I-Nor diamond from India Papa – and that huge sheet of paper, 2,500 feet long. And the elephant with the howdah. And the knife with eighty blades. And that huge vase from Russia.'

A cartoon showing an omnibus to the Great Exhibition. So many people wanted to board the buses that they were allowed to sit on the roof – the start of double-decker buses.

The Great Exhibition of all Nations ran from 1 May to 23 October 1851 and 6,201,856 people paid a visit. For the first three days the entrance fee was £1, expensive enough to ensure the rich had the exhibition to themselves. After this, fees dropped to 1 shilling (5p) from Mondays to Thursdays and ordinary people poured through the gates. Packed excursion trains, run by the railway companies, came from all over the country. Other travellers, like 85-year-old Mary Callinack from Penzance, walked to London!

Looking down the central aisle of the Crystal Palace.

Visitors were not disappointed. There were almost 100,000 objects of all kinds on show. About half were British but others came from as far as Egypt, Morocco, Bolivia, and Persia (Iran). Among the largest items were a steam hammer designed by Henry Nasmyth and the giant hydraulic jacks that had lifted the tubes of the Britannia Railway Bridge between Wales and Anglesey into place.

- The busiest day at the Great Exhibition was 13 October 1851. By 2 pm there were 92,000 visitors on site.

- Messrs Schweppes provided the catering. The best sellers were buns, soda water, lemonade and ginger beers. Ices were made on the spot from a steam powered freezing machine.

- Free public toilets were provided for the first time anywhere.

- The Great Exhibition made a profit of £186,000. The money was used to fund museums and colleges to improve art and design in Britain. These included the Victoria and Albert Museum in South Kensington.

SENDING A LETTER

Later, Laura wrote a long letter to her mother. She used a pen with a steel nib and a bottle of ink, drying her writing with a sheet of blotting paper. She stuck a penny stamp on the envelope. If the hotel messenger boy hurried to the post office, it would catch the last mail coach and be in her mother's hands in the morning.

The Victorians enjoyed a stunning change in the speed of communications, especially a better postal service. The Post Office had existed for hundreds of years, but the cost of sending a letter depended on how heavy it was and how far it was going. The charges were high and paid by the person who received the letter.

The General Post Office, London in 1849.

This picture from 1830 shows how mail was delivered by horse-drawn coach before the days of the train.

In 1840 Rowland Hill set up the 'penny post'. Letters could be sent anywhere for one old penny ($1/2$p). To prove they had paid, senders stuck a penny stamp on the envelope.

Most mail was sent by train, in mail coaches, and was sorted on the move. By the 1850s many letters were delivered the next day. By 1867, 642,000,000 letters were sent each year.

- Even quicker than the penny post was the telegraph. Messages were sent as electric signals along wires, often laid next to railway lines. In 1850 a telegraph cable was laid under the English Channel and the first messages were sent between London and Paris. In 1866 a cable 4,160 km long was laid under the Atlantic to Canada.

- William Cooke and Charles Wheatstone invented the telegraph in England in 1837. In 1840 American Samuel Morse invented Morse Code, a quick way of sending messages using a set of long and short signals for every letter of the alphabet.

- In 1876, Alexander Graham Bell, a Scot living in America, invented the telephone — a method of sending speech along wires. By 1879 there were telephone exchanges in London, Liverpool and Manchester.

A FASHIONABLE RESORT

The next day they caught the train to Brighton. 'We are staying at the queen of seaside resorts, my dear,' said Laura's father. That afternoon he hired a bathing machine for Laura and her governess to take a dip. Later they all dressed in their best clothes and joined the promenade. Everyone was on the seafront to see and be seen!

The most popular holiday for a Victorian family was a trip to the seaside. At first fashionable resorts like Brighton, Weymouth and Scarborough catered for upper-class and middle-class visitors who came for a health cure and a refined holiday. By the 1850s ordinary working people were beginning to visit the seaside on cheap train trips.

The Chain Pier and Marine Parade in Brighton around 1855.

A Victorian rhyme about a common peril in seaside hotels.

I am a bug, a seaside bug,
When folks in bed are lying snug,
About their skin we walk and creep,
And feast upon them while they sleep,
On lodging houses, where we breed
And at this season largely feed.

PUNCH · AND · JUDY

HAVE you a penny? well then, stay!
Haven't you any? don't go away!
Punch holds receptions all through the day,
Squeaking aloud to gather a crowd,
Scolding at Toby, beating his Wife,
Frightening the Constable out of his life,
And making jokes in a terrible passion,
As is Mr. Punch's peculiar fashion;
For this is his old, delightful plan
Of getting as many pence as he can.
   Then away he'll jog,
   With his Wife and his Dog,
   New folks to meet
   In the very next street.

Punch and Judy shows were always popular with children.

If the weather was warm, bathing was popular. Wealthier visitors, especially women, hired bathing machines for 1 shilling (5p). They provided a private place to change and were pulled by a horse to the water's edge. No resort was complete without a pier — the longer the better. The Chain Pier in Brighton, built like a suspension bridge, was opened in 1823. But it was soon outclassed by the West Pier, opened in 1866 and stretching 1,115 feet (340 metres) out to sea. Other seaside attractions included promenade concerts, troupes of pierrots (clowns), boat trips, Punch and Judy booths and donkey rides.

The Prince Regent's Pavilion set the exotic tone of Brighton. In the 1850s it was still a resort where a visitor could hope to see dukes and duchesses and even a prince or two.

GOING HOME

The days passed quickly and it was soon time to leave. They took the train to London, but Laura's father had one last treat in store, 'We are going home by steam packet,' he said. They hired a cab to the busy dockside and boarded *The Admiral* – a paddle steamer. 'What a perfect end to our journey,' thought Laura.

Steamboats on the Thames at Gravesend around 1835. In 1821 there were 188 steamers in service on short coastal voyages. By 1853 there were 639, many on ocean routes.

When Victorians proudly sang the patriotic song 'Rule Britannia, Britannia rules the waves,' it wasn't an empty boast. Ever since the Battle of Trafalgar in 1805 the Royal Navy had been unchallenged at sea. But more importantly, Britain was the leading shipbuilding nation in the world and by 1900 British ships carried almost half of the world's trade.

Ships changed rapidly during Victorian times. In 1837 most were still made of wood and powered by sails. Sensible people thought iron ships would fall apart in a storm or steam engines break down on a long voyage. Then Isambard Kingdom Brunel built two ships that proved them wrong.

28

The SS *Great Britain* in rough seas. In September 1846 she showed how strong iron ships could be. She ran aground in Dundram Bay, Ireland, and withstood months of storms before being refloated in August 1847.

The first was the *Great Western* — a wooden vessel with a steam engine driving paddle wheels. In 1838 she crossed the Atlantic in 14 days without any problems. His second ship, the *Great Britain* was launched in 1843. She was made of iron and driven by a propeller.

(*Right*) Steam vessels available from London to Newcastle, 1874.

HERMITAGE STEAM WHARF,
Wapping High street,
J. A. Clinkshill, whartinger.

Steam Vessels to	Ships	Masters
EDINBURGH, Leith, Glasgow & Greenock		
One of the following screw steamers of the London & Edinburgh Shipping Company every Wednesday & Saturday, taking passengers & goods for all parts of Scotland.	Marmion .... .T. Raison Iona .... .R. C. Hossack Morna .... .A. Howling Oscar .... .J. Hutchison Staffa .... .James Lamb	

For particulars apply at the Wharf

NEWCASTLE-ON-TYNE		
One of the following screw steamers of the Tyne Steam Shipping Co. every Wednesday & Saturday evening at 6, with passengers & goods for all parts of the north of England.	C. M. Palmer .... .Cay Earl Percy .... .Geddes Grenadier .... .Newton Admiral ....————	

For particulars apply to Alfred T. Bigg, at the Wharf

Laura's last view of London was from the busy River Thames.

TIMELINE

1837 — On the death of her uncle, William IV, Princess Victoria is crowned queen. Charles Dickens publishes *Oliver Twist*.

1838 — The London to Birmingham Railway opened.

1840 — Queen Victoria marries Prince Albert. The Post Master, Rowland Hill, introduces the 'penny post'.

1842 — The Mines Act bans women and children younger than 10 from working underground.

1842-6 — The Great Famine in Ireland.

1844 — Co-op starts in Rochdale.

1848 — Cholera outbreak kills 53,000 people. First Public Health Act.

1851 — The Great Exhibition is held at the Crystal Palace in London, to show the wonders of British industry to the world. The census shows more people living in towns than in the country.

1854 — War with Russia in the Crimea. Florence Nightingale leads a team of nurses.

1856 — Henry Bessemer's converter halves the cost of steel production.

1857 — Indians revolt against British rule. The rebellion is ruthlessly crushed.

1858 — Queen Victoria is crowned Empress of India.

1859 — Charles Darwin publishes his book on evolution, *On the Origin of Species.*

1861 — Prince Albert dies from typhoid fever. Queen Victoria begins a lifetime of mourning.

1865 — The Red Flag Acts cut the speed of 'horseless carriages' to 2 mph in towns.

1866 — A telegraph cable 2,500 miles (4,160km) long is laid under the Atlantic Ocean.

1869 — The first Sainsbury's shop opens.

1870 — School Boards set up to build schools if there is a shortage of places.

1872 — First FA Cup played – Wanderers 1, Royal Engineers 0.

1875 — Second Public Health Act. All town councils have to provide a clean water supply and drainage.

1875 — Captain Webb becomes the first person to swim the English Channel – 40 miles in 22 hours.

1876 — Alexander Graham Bell invents the telephone.

1877 — William Booth sets up the Salvation Army in London.

1882 — Women allowed to keep their own property when they marry.

1884 — All men who owned or rented houses allowed to vote. Charles Parsons invents the steam turbine.

1885 — First electric trams run in British cities.

1887 — Queen Victoria celebrates 50 years as monarch.

1890 — The Forth Rail Bridge – the longest railway bridge in the world (1,700 feet – 520 m) is opened in Scotland.

1892 — Keir Hardie elected as MP for West Ham – the first 'Labour Party' MP.

1899 — Asprin invented.

1901 — Queen Victoria dies, age 81, on the Isle of Wight. She is succeeded by her son Edward VII.

GLOSSARY

Arabian Nights — Fairy tales from the Middle East.

ballad — Song with a story.

barouche — A double-seated four-wheeled carriage.

Britannia Railway Bridge — Built by Robert Stephenson from Wales to Anglesey. Opened in 1850, the trains ran inside huge iron tubes 30m above the sea.

carriage people — A Victorian saying for wealthy and respectable people. Shopkeepers valued customers like this and called them the 'carriage trade'.

cholera — A disease that causes terrible sickness and diarrhoea. A person can lose so much water from their bodies that they die.

class — Victorian society was deeply divided. People thought of themselves as upper class, middle class or working class.

counting houses — Places where businessmen kept their accounts (records to do with money).

crossing sweeping — Sweeping the roads so that richer people could cross without getting dirty.

cutting — Channel for railway tracks cut through high ground.

empire — The lands governed by one country.

excavation — Digging.

gauge — Width of the railway track.

gig — A light two-wheeled carriage.

girders — Large iron beams.

governess — A private teacher and companion.

harness — Equipment fastening the horse to the carriage.

housemaids — Servants who cleaned the house.

howdah — Seat and canopy on the back of an elephant.

hydraulic jacks — Water-powered machines for lifting heavy weights.

nurserymaids — Servants who looked after children.

points — Switchgear to move trains from one track to another.

promenade — A walk taken to look at other people and how they are dressed, also a paved public walk, especially one along a seafront.

rope works — A factory for making ropes.

sash bars — Iron bars that held the glass in windows.

signal — A mechanism to tell the train driver to stop, slow down or carry on.

specifications — Plans and measurements.

steam packet — Regular steamship service.

technological — Using science and industry.

trusses — Supports.

typhoid — A highly infectious fever that could kill children and adults.

valet — A personal servant for a gentleman.

vendor — Salesperson.

viaduct — A bridge for a railway.

FURTHER READING

All About the Industrial Revolution by Peter Hepplewhite, Hodder Wayland, 2002
From Workshop to Empire Britain 1750-1900 by Hamish Macdonald, Stanley Thornes, 1995
The History Detective Investigates: Victorian Transport by Colin Stott, Hodder Wayland, 2003

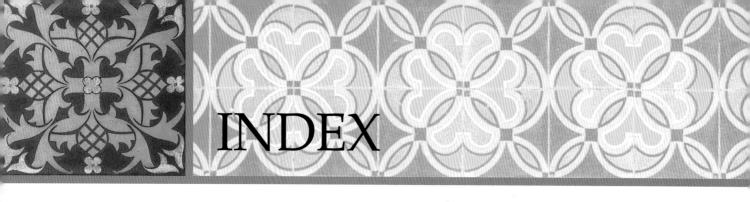

INDEX